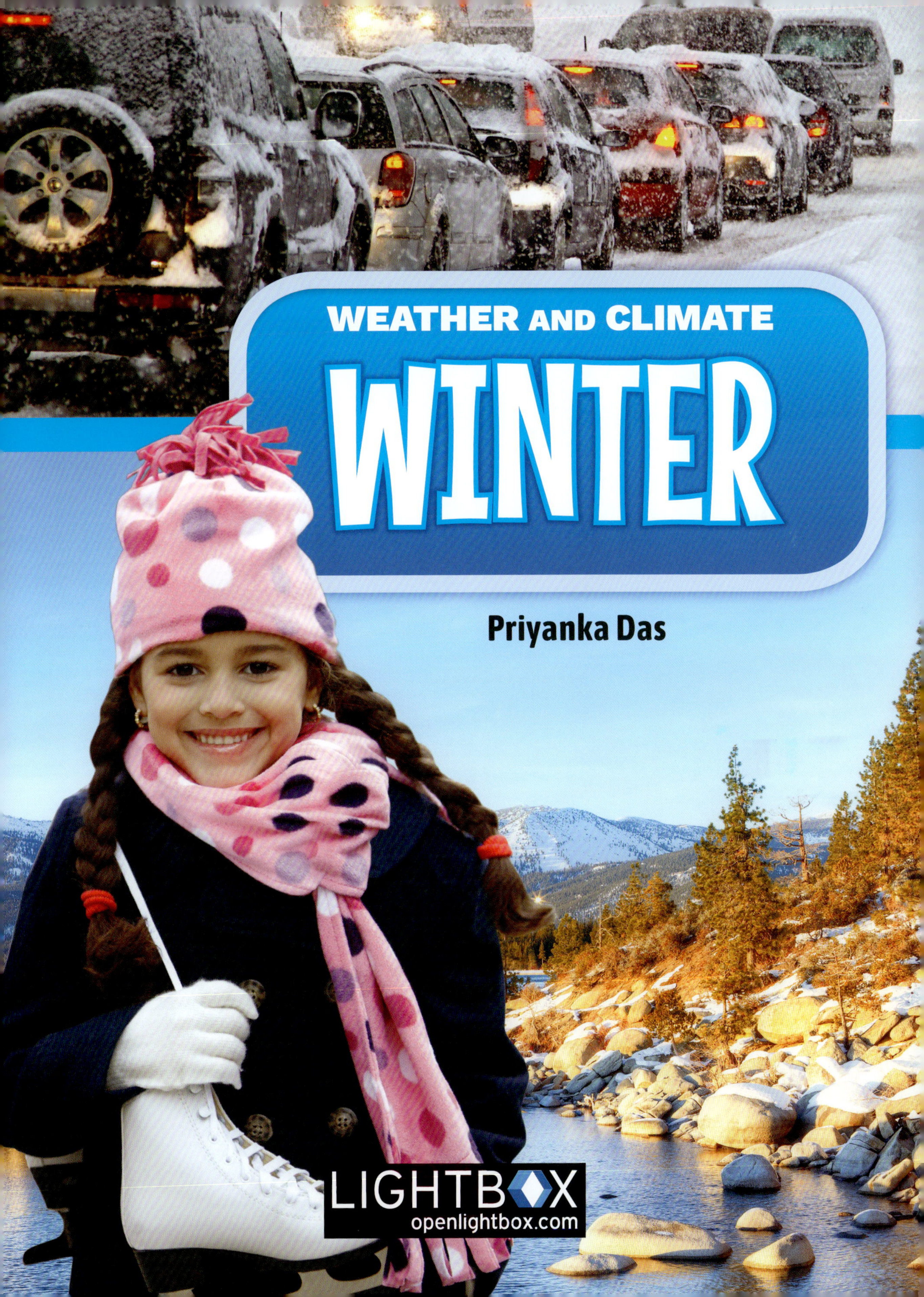
WEATHER AND CLIMATE
WINTER
Priyanka Das
LIGHTBOX
openlightbox.com

LIGHTBOX

Go to **www.openlightbox.com** and enter this book's unique code.

ACCESS CODE

LBXQ7422

Lightbox is an all-inclusive digital solution for the teaching and learning of curriculum topics in an original, groundbreaking way. Lightbox is based on National Curriculum Standards.

STANDARD FEATURES OF LIGHTBOX

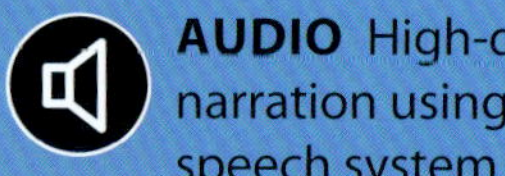

AUDIO High-quality narration using text-to-speech system

ACTIVITIES Printable PDFs that can be emailed and graded

SLIDESHOWS Pictorial overviews of key concepts

VIDEOS Embedded high-definition video clips

WEBLINKS Curated links to external, child-safe resources

TRANSPARENCIES Step-by-step layering of maps, diagrams, charts, and timelines

INTERACTIVE MAPS Interactive maps and aerial satellite imagery

QUIZZES Ten multiple choice questions that are automatically graded and emailed for teacher assessment

KEY WORDS Matching key concepts to their definitions

Contents

Wonderful Wintertime

The weather becomes colder. Snow starts to fall. Winter has arrived.

Every winter, some bears find a comfortable den to sleep in. They often go to sleep for months. Other animals play during winter. River otters slide down snowy hills for fun.

How do you spend your winter? Are you and your friends learning to ice-skate or ski? Maybe your family goes on dogsled rides. Winter is the best time for these activities.

If you live in a warm place, winter may not be very cold. Snow might not fall. Perhaps you spend your winter surfing or flying kites. Imagine how your perfect winter would look.

Winter in the United States

Winter usually lasts from December to February. The weather is different across the 50 states. Most northern states have colder winters than the southern states.

HAWAI'I
Hawai'i has the hottest winters in the United States. People often go surfing here in winter.

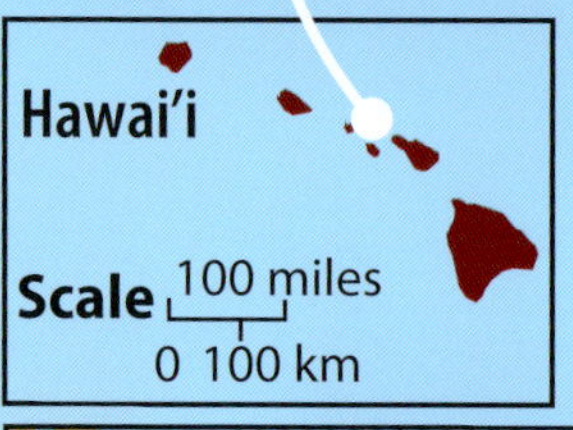

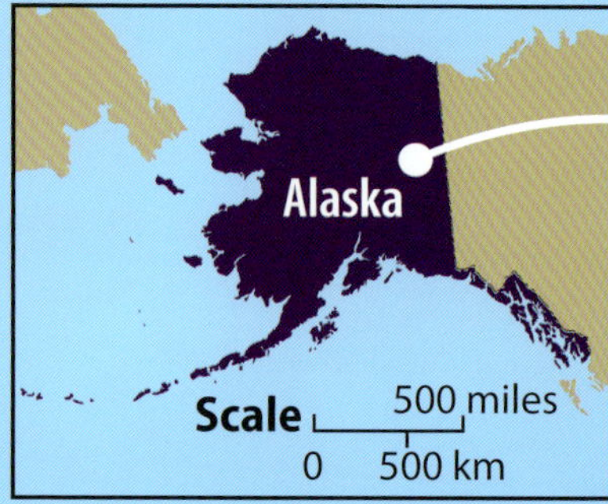

ALASKA
Alaska is colder than any other state. Parts of Alaska are covered in ice all year.

WASHINGTON
Washington's highest mountain is called Mount Rainier. It is the snowiest place in the United States.

Can You Find Your State?

Find your state on the map. What color is it? Find the same color in the legend.

What is the average temperature of your state in winter?

Legend

Degrees Fahrenheit (°F)

- 0–10
- 10–15
- 15–20
- 20–25
- 25–30
- 30–35
- 35–40
- 40–45
- 45–50
- 50–55
- 55–60
- 60–70
- Water
- Other countries

Scale 0 250 miles 250 km

The Weather in Winter

Often, the same kind of weather happens at about the same time each year. These weather patterns are the four seasons. Seasons change as Earth travels around the Sun. Earth's journey around the Sun takes one year. As Earth moves, half of it tilts, or leans, toward the Sun. The opposite side tilts away.

Around December, Earth's Northern **Hemisphere** tilts away from the Sun. It receives less of the Sun's heat and energy. This is when winter begins in the United States. Winter is the coldest season of the year. It has the fewest hours of sunlight, too. Snow falls in parts of the United States and other countries.

Winter in the Northern Hemisphere

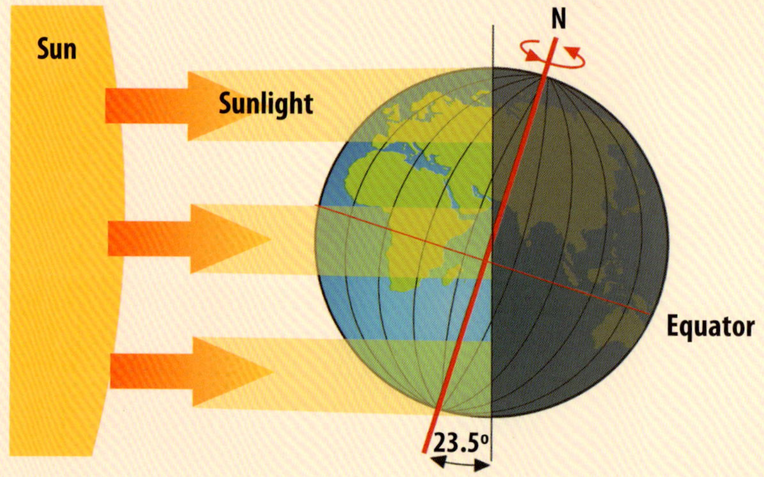

An Average Winter Season

From December to February, there are about 700 hours of sunshine in San Diego, California.

Approximately how many hours of sunshine does Tampa get in a winter season? What about Syracuse and Dallas?

Which of these four states has the most rain and snow in winter? Which has the least?

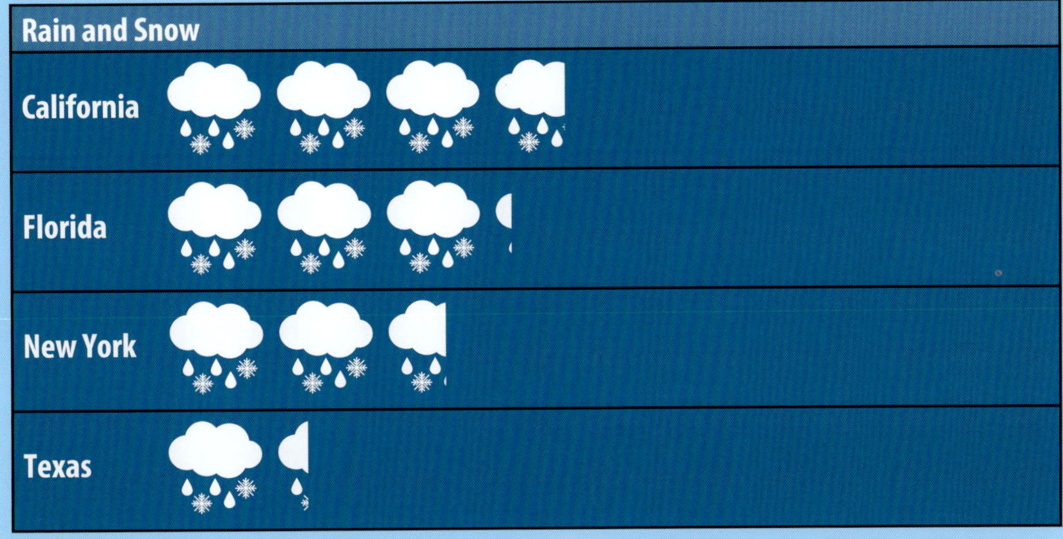

= 100 hours

= 1 inch (2.5 centimeters)

Blizzards sometimes blow in without warning. A blizzard can quickly bury areas in snow, trapping people out in the cold.

Extreme Winter

Winters can be extreme. Temperatures become very cold. There is heavy snowfall. People face dangers in this weather.

BLIZZARDS

Blizzards are big snowstorms with strong winds. The amount of snow in the air makes it hard to see outside. It can be difficult for cars, trucks, or buses to drive. Schools, businesses, and even cities may shut down.

ICY ROADS

When roads are covered with snow and ice, they become slippery. Vehicles slip more often. Drivers sometimes have accidents.

FREEZING TEMPERATURES

Being outside in freezing weather is dangerous for people and pets. **Frostbite** is possible. Low temperatures can also cause **hypothermia**. It is important to dress warmly.

Extreme Winter Timeline

Extreme winters bring snowstorms and record temperatures. The United States has had many extreme winters.

February 1899
Florida has one of the heaviest snowfalls in its history.

Winter 1936
North Dakota, South Dakota, Minnesota, and Iowa have their coldest recorded winter.

January 1971
The temperature in central Alaska is -79.8°F (-62.1° Celsius). This is the coldest it has ever been in the United States.

March 1993
The "Storm of the Century" strikes the U.S. East Coast. The damage from blizzards costs about $5.5 billion.

February 2013
The northeastern United States is hit by Nemo, a huge blizzard. More than 2 feet (0.6 meters) of snow falls in some places.

February 2019
There is a snowstorm in a Hawai'i state park. It may be the first time snow has fallen here.

Weather Tools over Time

Weather is often hard to **predict**. That has not stopped people from trying. Thousands of years ago, humans studied clouds. Cloud patterns helped them guess what weather was coming next. Modern technology is more advanced. It took a long time to develop the weather tools used today.

THERMOMETER

A thermometer measures temperature. It can tell people if the air is hot or cold. **Mercury** in the thermometer expands with heat. The higher the temperature, the more it expands.

Galileo Galilei was an astronomer. In the late 1500s, he invented a device that could show differences in temperature.

BAROMETER

A barometer measures the weight of the air. The weight of air changes weather. Lighter air can mean rain, wind, or clouds are coming. Heavier air may mean fewer clouds and cool, dry air.

Evangelista Torricelli invented the barometer in 1643. He was a physicist.

WEATHER SATELLITE

A weather satellite takes pictures of Earth from space. It collects information about temperature and cloud patterns. Meteorologists use this information to predict the weather each day. This is called weather forecasting.

In 1960, TIROS-1 became the first weather satellite to work in space.

Discover Scientists

Scientists want to understand the world around us. They try to find out why things happen. You can be a scientist, too. Learn about what different kinds of scientists do.

Astronomers study stars and outer space.

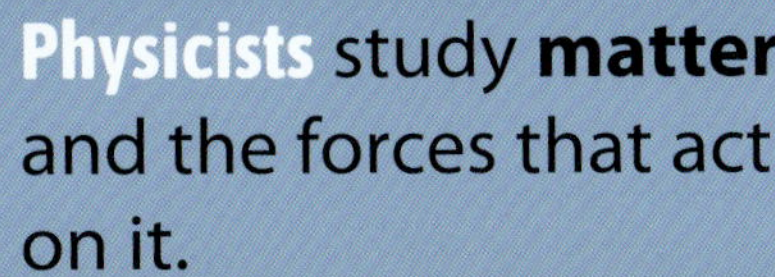

Physicists study **matter** and the forces that act on it.

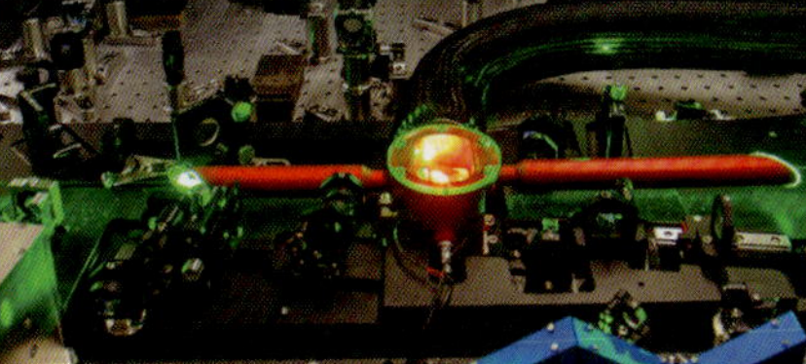

Meteorologists study and predict the weather.

Winter Technology Today

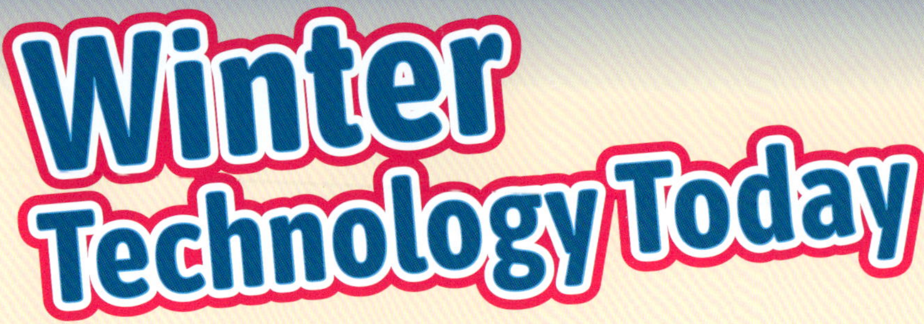

Scientists find creative ways to make winter easier. Some technology improves safety. Other inventions make people more comfortable.

SNOW REMOVAL VEHICLES

Snow removal vehicles clear snow and ice from roads. People with special training drive them. Some snow removal vehicles can even drive themselves.

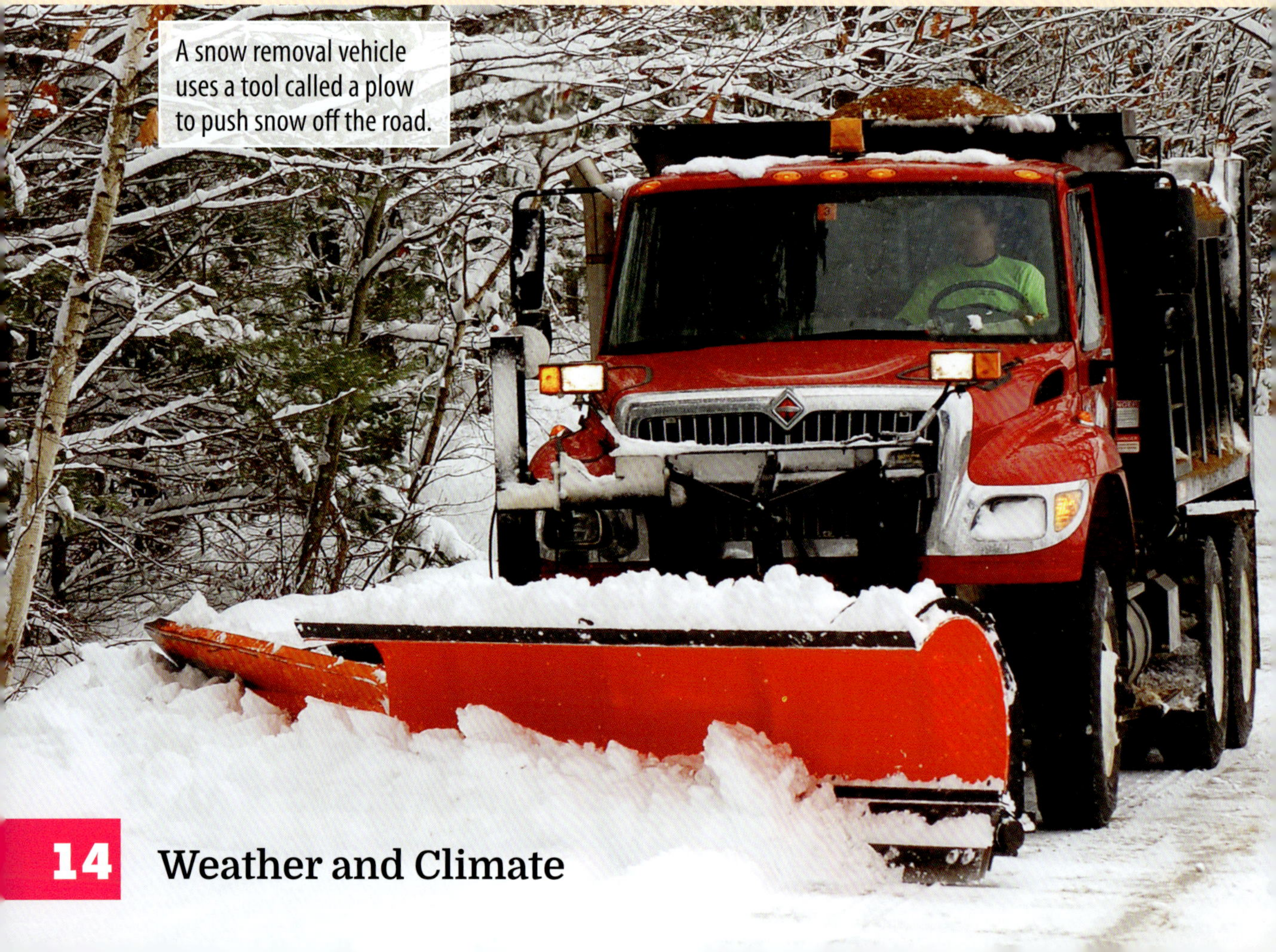

A snow removal vehicle uses a tool called a plow to push snow off the road.

SOLAR-POWERED ROADS

Solar-powered roads do not become icy. They can remove snow by melting it. This type of road is powered by the Sun's energy. It has **solar panels** that convert sunlight into heat and electricity.

The world's first solar-powered road was built in Normandy, France, in 2016.

TOUCHSCREEN GLOVES

Smartphones do not work with regular gloves. Touchscreen gloves help people use phones in cold weather.

Touchscreen gloves transfer electricity from the finger to the smartphone's screen.

A Home for a Cold Climate

There are some cities and towns that become very cold every winter. Temperatures may be low all year, too. Houses in these areas are built to face the dangers of a cold **climate**.

Triple-pane windows

Triple-pane windows have three panes, or sheets of glass, that are separated by air. These windows keep heat inside the house. The house stays warm.

Sloped roof

Snow can pile up on the roof. This adds a dangerous amount of weight. The roof might **collapse**. A roof with sloping sides lets snow slide down to the ground.

Insulation

Insulating materials block heat from passing through. The walls and roof should be lined with insulation. This keeps heat from leaving the house.

Covered entrances

A cover over the entrances protects people from snow or blizzards.

A **thermostat** helps control the temperature in a house. **Warren Johnson** invented the electric thermostat in **1883**.

The **smart thermostat** was invented in **2009**. It uses the internet to change the temperature.

Blizzard Safety

Being outside in a blizzard is dangerous. People may have to stay in the house for a long time. The power could go out. Electricity and heating systems can stop working. To prepare for a blizzard, keep supplies at home. Store water, food, warm clothes, and blankets.

If it is necessary to go out, wear warm clothes. Other **accessories** also help during a blizzard.

A warm hat stops body heat from escaping through the head.

Goggles protect the eyes from snow and ice.

A face mask covers the mouth. This stops very cold air from entering the lungs.

Dress for the Weather

Use the weather forecast to help you choose what to wear.

1. Find the weather forecast for your city or town. What is the temperature going to be?
2. Match the temperature to the chart below.
3. Go to your closet. Find the right outfit to wear tomorrow.

Temperature	Tops	Bottoms	Footwear	Accessories
77°F and above (25°C and above)			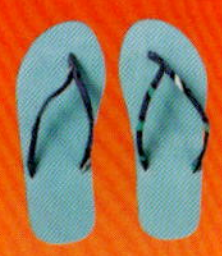	
70°F–77°F (21°C–25°C)		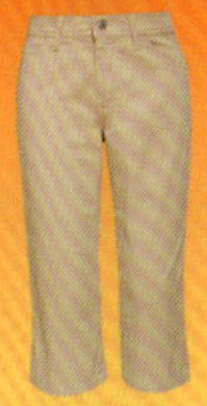		
50°F–70°F (10°C–21°C)		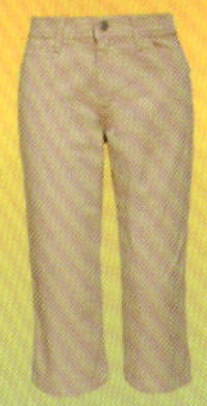		
32°F–50°F (0°C–10°C)				
32°F and below (0°C and below)				

Winter around the World

POLAR CLIMATE ZONE

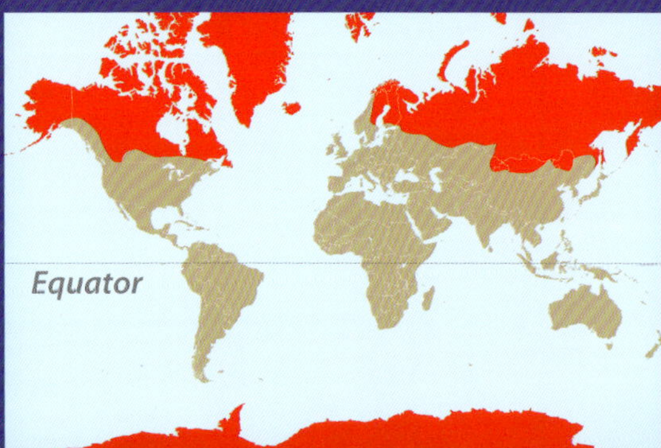

The polar zone is the coldest climate zone. It has very long, cold, dark winters. Parts of this zone are covered in ice all year. Each month has an average temperature colder than 50°F (10°C).

Wildlife: Arctic Fox, Arctic Wolf, Penguin, Polar Bear

TEMPERATE CLIMATE ZONE

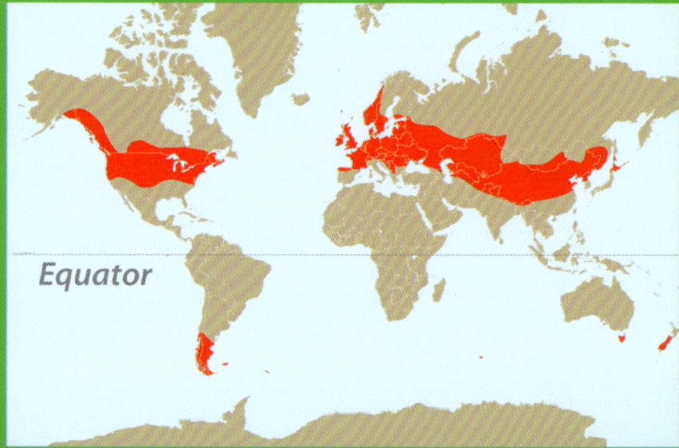

The temperate zone has four very different seasons. These are winter, spring, summer, and fall. Winters are cold in temperate climates. Temperatures change **significantly** between summer and winter.

Wildlife: Giant Panda, Raccoon, Red Fox, Squirrel

Winter is different around the world. An imaginary line called the equator circles Earth, dividing it into two halves. Places close to the equator are often hot all year. Areas far from the equator are cold. Earth has four major climate zones.

SUBTROPICAL CLIMATE ZONE

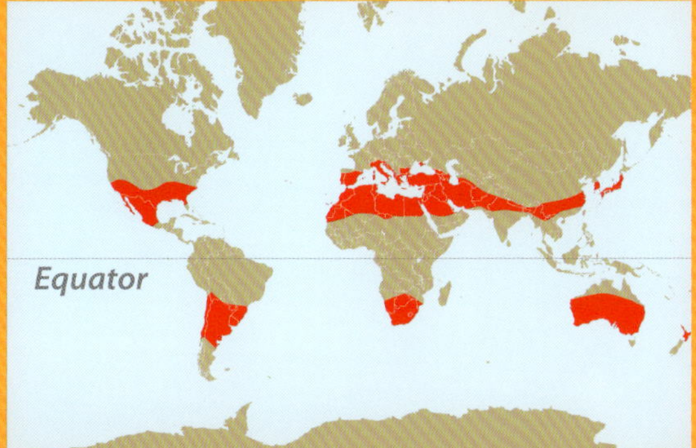

The subtropical zone has a warm or hot climate. The weather in winter is mild or cool. Frost and snowfall are rare. In some areas, it rains during winter.

Wildlife: Alligator, Kangaroo, Leopard, Python

TROPICAL CLIMATE ZONE

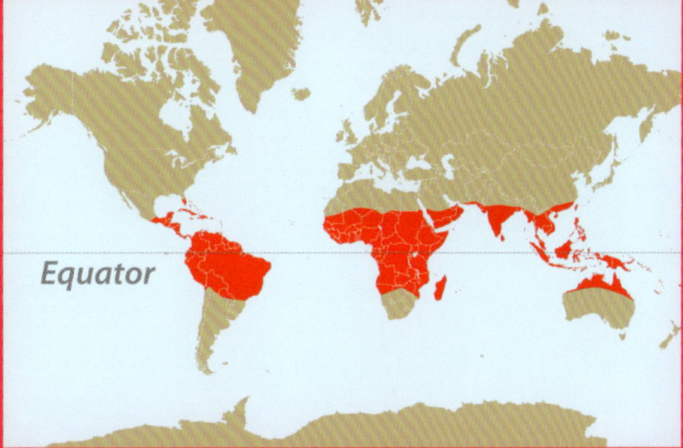

The tropical zone is the hottest climate zone. The weather is hot all year. Every month's average temperature is warmer than 64°F (18°C). There are heavy rains and almost no snow. In some parts of this zone, winter is a dry season.

Wildlife: Gorilla, Komodo Dragon, Orangutan, Rhinoceros

Quiz

1 Which instrument measures the weight of air?

A: A barometer

2 When does the northern half of Earth tilt away from the Sun?

A: Around December

3 Which is the coldest U.S. state?

A: Alaska

4 What is a blizzard?

A: A big snowstorm with strong winds

5 What are two dangers that people and pets face in freezing temperatures?

A: Frostbite and hypothermia

6 What are some animals that live in the polar climate zone?

A: Arctic fox, arctic wolf, penguin, and polar bear

7 What was the name of the first weather satellite to work in space?

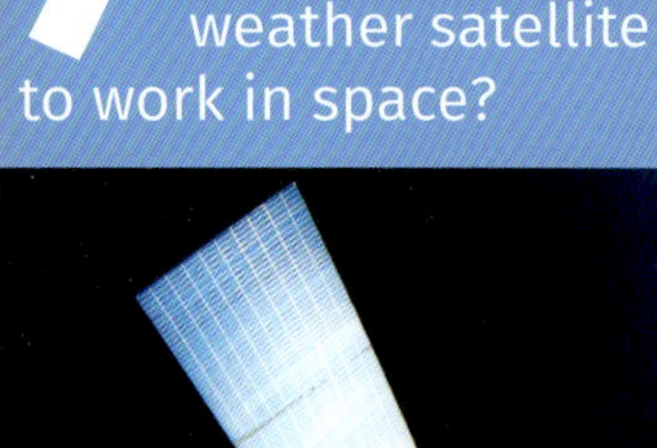

A: TIROS-1

8 What type of roads are powered by the Sun's energy?

A: Solar-powered roads

9 What type of scientist studies and predicts the weather?

A: A meteorologist

10 What device is used to control the temperature in a house?

A: A thermostat

Key Words

accessories: items that are worn or carried in addition to the main outfit

climate: the average weather of an area over a period of time

collapse: to break apart and fall down suddenly

frostbite: damage to skin and other body parts caused by freezing

hemisphere: one of two halves of Earth, especially above or below the equator

hypothermia: a condition in which the temperature of the body is dangerously low

matter: any object that has mass and takes up space

mercury: a silver metal that is liquid at room temperature

predict: to say that something will happen in the future

significantly: by a large amount or in a way that is easy to notice

solar panels: flat, rectangular devices with units called photovoltaic cells that use the Sun's light to create electricity

Index

LIGHTBOX

SUPPLEMENTARY RESOURCES

Click on the plus icon found in the bottom left corner of each spread to open additional teacher resources.

- Download and print the book's quizzes and activities
- Access curriculum correlations
- Explore additional web applications that enhance the Lightbox experience

LIGHTBOX DIGITAL TITLES
Packed full of integrated media

VIDEOS

INTERACTIVE MAPS

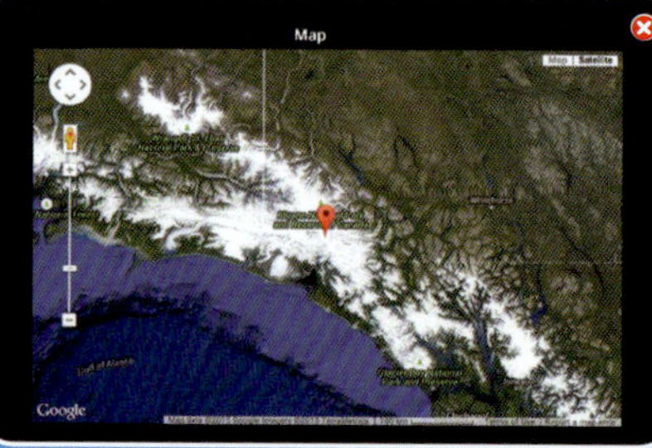

WEBLINKS

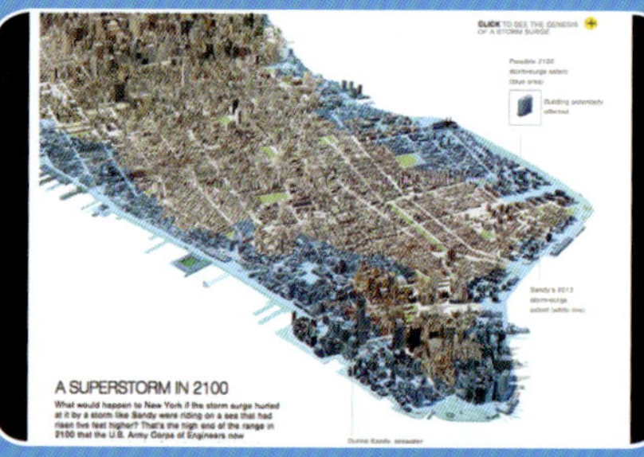

SLIDESHOWS

QUIZZES

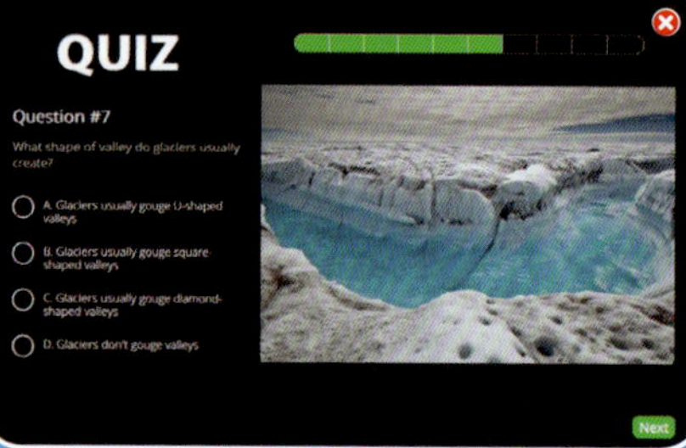

OPTIMIZED FOR

- ✔ TABLETS
- ✔ WHITEBOARDS
- ✔ COMPUTERS
- ✔ AND MUCH MORE!

Published by Smartbook Media Inc.
350 5th Avenue, 59th Floor New York, NY 10118
Website: www.openlightbox.com

Library of Congress Control Number: 2019942193

ISBN 978-1-5105-4512-0 (hardcover)
ISBN 978-1-5105-4513-7 (multi-user eBook)

Printed in Guangzhou, China
1 2 3 4 5 6 7 8 9 0 23 22 21 20 19

062019
122718

Project Coordinator: Priyanka Das
Designer: Ana María Vidal

Photo Credits
Every reasonable effort has been made to trace ownership and to obtain permission to reprint copyright material. The publisher would be pleased to have any errors or omissions brought to its attention so that they may be corrected in subsequent printings. The publisher acknowledges Getty Images, iStock, Shutterstock, Alamy, Newscom, and Dreamstime as its primary image suppliers for this title.